Gnashing Teeth Publishing
242 East Main Street
Norman AR 71960

Printed in the United States of America

ISBN 979-8-9875694-9-8

Library of Congress Control Number: 2024930454

Non-Fiction: Poetry

Gnashing Teeth Publishing First Edition

Excavator

§

Joshua Bridgwater Hamilton

For Letty

And in memory of
James Edward Hamilton

§ GEOGRAPHIES

The rapacious curve of Southern Texas
sucks buoyancy from cloud, storm,
cetaceous billow of wind and pre-
cipitation. Far from the Ohio Valley,
Smokies, green dreams - closer
than we think to San
Salvador: heat stretches my body, memory
melts thin & stringy in a taffy dance
where twists of mesquite
ravage dogwood & maple,
hot judgement tears from a throat
of sand and petrol, the public scavenges
from the creases between private
domains, while beneath
dewy corpses of quetzalcoatlus,
adelobasileus, alamosaurus, cypress,
gingko, and palm press into quarts
and radiate holistic energies
from the exhaust of our internal
combustions: secure my supply
of magnolia blooms,
honeysuckle disguised
as pungent mead, feed through holes
in a habitation of excoriating rust,
and the poison mold growing
in the water filter. Slow disappear
of a body's fortitude while beyond
the southern suburbs bodies move
through scrubby atmosphere
flattened against sunset.
Come for me, but beware: these neighbors
keep vigilant; I'll plant keys
in the watery roots of all

the sibilant bird-of-paradise bushes.
Come in to find our floors bare, nothing
stands in the shadowed corners,
my daughter will bring trays
of ice and water, the only two cats
rubbing the loss of concrete
and wood to slowest economy.
No matter — you can stay
forever against our cold history's
cadaver. We speak an argot
we ourselves cannot comprehend
and soon from the ardent
well of apprehension
the armed community clambers forth
to congregate in pools
of security lights
striving to conjugate their fear
into comprehensible verb forms.
Help us articulate
something besides barbs
and wires; help us excavate
past sediment, strata, lines
confining one language and
one epoch
from another.

The morning moon pales
in the parchment sky,
its mistaken hour belling
insomniac obsessions.

Far from somnolent pulse
of aqueous dark and ocean-
floor hush, the moon
etches its blanched lunarscape
onto calm coasts and fields
where all lie still
and slumber witless.

Plastic life stamped out of mold –
sleek black and glinting white
stuffed with chips and circuits –
detunes so slightly
with each revolution:
microscopic wear
in the machinery.

A high-pressure system
frames the viewer,
cloud animus that defines
by outline — one wispy
moon-eye, milk-shot
in the middle of day, blinded
and lost in the land of brilliant
sweeping algorithms, precise payment plan:
a landscape of strip mall, field,
road and restaurant
where the pimple and crease of each expression
moves with the sharp, flat
lack of confusion.

for Robin Carstensen

At the edge where the last
shallow shelf pans out,
slipping its melted glass
up over the swath of beach,
my feet merge with shattered
shell: the earth's thin line
between ancient hydraulic pressures
that accumulate, pummel, transform
matter and time
with the force of the gulf
behind each heave.

Just inches away
roasting vacation bodies
absorb kilowatts of solar
and aural energies, lift fractured conches
to the ear, suck up the sound
and take it with them into their vehicles
and home: masters of metal
and economy, out on highways
plowing metric tons of technology
into each other—small, soft pilots
that can tear apart
millennial sediments so suddenly
with their constant smudge of humanity.

When I step down and in
I see the water
flash away from shore,
blurring the landscape of shell
with aerated water

and roiled sand.
In a split second
exposed to sun
shells snap into sharp relief.

Another wave, the blurred scene,
then just in the heave
a suspension
at the kinetic apex:
the sediment settles
the surf freezes its tranquil pane
and the iridescent wreck of marine life
dials into lucid focus—
full and limpid with the lens of aquatic optics
translating the seafloor topography
into an instantaneous wonderment of detail.

A quick sigh
and ancient, timeless force
wipes out the painstaking
still life—one
in a day's millions.

I slop back to the beach towel
around which my family
has erected tents, chairs, over-
stuffed coolers; I grab a beer
and heave my worn, burnt body
onto the waiting terry cloth.

Sabal palmettos point wispy eyes at sky
and dream cloud scuds as closing arguments
against the salt-bitten heat.
Pluck their terminal buds,
taste them transform into
hearts of palm as you crush
meat between molars: tender harvest
that kills the tree. Because of this
they grow so tall, unfold
vital organs to the secret sun.

The anacahuita, however, sheds
fleshy blooms like an abundant
white sadness lost in seasons'
borders, petals
filling the lawn with their soft flames.
If you pick the olive-shaped fruits
eat them one by one
sweet dizziness enters the tongue
unwraps balance from the surface
of your spine, releases fickle attentions,
melancholia, precari-
ousness, and emotions
of uncertainty
to roam the body
until it forgets
the limits of its own
definition until
it becomes
some
        body
                else.

When you find
the cool mauve
of phanera purpurea, the swelling
in your mind begins to ease, ulcered
walls regain shape, soft lily
flowers press skin and draw
deep violet from flesh
into sparkling plant cells.
These bright butterflies
named alibangbang in the Philippines
leap into heavy summer shadow
where violence as much as joy
languish in each other's sweltering
thick arms, magenta flashes
dart between the limbs
and draw your troubled
mind out into
the searing
light.

for all the Moons and Stripes

The dream dial clicked
and a snow channel fades
from tubed memory
into shadowboxed movement.

Dim hours sketch details
of our miniature cathedrals.
Down the hall, room
after room appears.

Coffee steams a pod version of roast;
patio and driveway collect pools
of luminous fog,

                  trace

tall sienna fencing, sway-back
palm trees, collection
of metal frames de-
installed and scattered

                 over pavement
like theologies.

Sleek movement begins
at yard edges: through the
fencing, incomprehensible
residence, under-
growth, shimmery fields where lawn

translates lawn. Cats materialize
from their wooded portals

when I whistle and rattle

the kibble, invoke
the dawn to just
come on
                    and so

softly they appear
that I think of night

as day lifts instinct and nature
above the cats' sinewy pace,
knotting flank and fur

into a hypnotist's rhythm,
their language of purrs punctuated
by irritated hiss – day
                              lifting

all the measured anchor points
of suburban pathology

beyond the roofs, the palms
where people mark

the undefined gray matter
with their territories, lifts

the gridded canvas
of grid into
the unwritten
                    feline
lifted
        sky.

for Marti Bingham

I.

We measure
the giraffe's neck
in yards,
its cantilevered
gallop seems to
defy physics –

AB, Aunt M, and I
queue before the
savanna enclosure,
admire in lassitude
the awkward
fluency:

Between gallops
evening slides
open its
window, lets in
cool air.

For 3 bucks
the zookeeper
relinquishes
greened-up
lettuce:
we step
into ritual:
prehensile
tongue connects

12

nature and human
gesture.

AB delights
at the leafy
offering
counters
my skepticism
at the complex
fact of the giraffe
standing before us.

II.

Later, in the canary cage
the three of us –
daughter,
          father,
                    aunt —
revel in the twitchy
syntax
      of songbirds –
lilting
      arpeggios
and staccato notation

recall ancient instincts
                    migrations
          kindlings
lemon-yellow
          lightning prayers
that balm the loss my aunt
and I suffer

in ages
        technologies
                gods.

Aunt M wonders
if they're canaries
            or parakeets?
    While we correct
each other,
AB runs through
        the aviary
collecting color
            and sound.

Afternoon's long chronology
pares us into thirds:

heat   thirst   weariness

drive us further into singular
perceptions: the zoo,

I see from its riot-color map,
was built for circular time
                and movement:
one moment's genus
            sliding into
                    the next
and we
        three
            generations
step right into
            its fluid
logic.

also for Marti Bingham

Summer covered Tennessee
in its wavering sheet of incendiary
all cooked yellows and browns
beneath blown-out folds of green —
the sky a bright, suspended billow
pierced by rocket-tips.
Nineteen eighty something
I wore socks to the knee,
soccer t-shirt tucked into waist —
we drove down the high shimmer
to Knoxville, to visit Aunt Marti.

She was still married then to Larry,
and they lived in a low, skinny house
full of love, psychology,
thick cream of blooms
and a garage full of motorcycle.

While adults talked softly
among the high pile carpet
and wood paneled walls,
I played in the empty green
rectangle of yard framed
in fence. I hunted slug
and beetle as the chain-link
tilted afternoon askew.

Sometime during earth's nervous tilt
I slipped into the kitchen
and grabbed a purple-bright
packet of Kool-Aid,

15

snuck it out
into the sapphire and camouflage
of afternoon.

I was about to learn
that higher tides and roaring gales
surge from our carpeted, lamp-
lit securities, blindside and shift
the contours of desire —
that finding a castaway boat
does not mean you can save it,
even when it's your own.

I ripped the flat, gritty envelope,
shook a serving-size dose
of distilled day-glow crystals
into mouth and a conduit
of energy opened: I tasted
evening as it burst wide
open its colossal,
technicolor kraken.

Mi amor es paso, tránsito, larga muerte gustada
Federico García Lorca

Sun spotlights the measured pass of hours:
slow wilt of alcohol and tobacco
in the bare oven of a box house
in sub-tropical Texas.

Rhythm of detergent paint-dripped
across enamel basket, sough of rumpled cloth,
door bang and pump, the soiled weight
under salt-stained sun.
Water flows and wash
cycles time through wobbly sprints of forenoon work.

Over worn sink, traced delicate in calcium,
last blast of morning catches me
full in the face as it escapes
above the garage and beyond
the rented house.

Here, buzzed present
stills the consequence of choice—
its chain of command
a seductive past
loosening cocaine grips,
blinding nights;
pyrrhic freedoms fade softly
into heat of noon sweat.

The compost can leaks rich,
heavy dankness
past the knocking laundry room

out into backyard—
the trowel churns dirt
as peels, rinds, and eggshells
tumble into the loamy
brown mouth. For a second,
dripping, I see a mirage:
all my broken parts swallowed
into cool, dirty wholeness.

Someone found the body by a cotton gin
near Chapman Ranch. In the fall
cotton balls tumble and clump
like wet snow on the flat Texas roads.
The summer sits on a plush throne
of autumn, wears a bright, plastic
crown. Expect Hanna to make
landfall noon on Saturday –
80-100 mph winds
stroke the face of Gulf waters –
foil pressed onto brushed metal.
They called the Rangers in to assist
with the investigation – the black
bear sleeping in a kiddie pool,
protesters heckling staff
leaving the Chinese consulate,
slate morning dawning on the straight line
leathered skin makes with a harvested field.
An iron grating leaves a scarlet
silhouette. Dressed up in clothes
left by patrons of their 70 year
laundry business, Chang Wan-Ji
and Han Sho-er become viral
Instagram models. The white
umbrella opens over carmine
cellophane. Storm surge floods
the Art Museum first floor
and parts of downtown. A protester
is shot and killed in Austin. A DNA
study shows widespread impact
of African slave trade. The wind
enters the trees.

for Dorothy Black

The green and black field
spreads days out
like a radar scope
pinging 4o years deep –
if you steer the submarine
North by Northeast
till you hit 85° 22' 5g" W

                    38° 44' 1o" N

the tectonic fissures in time's cortex
will expand from blinding light
as waves of desire swallow
hull and crew whole –
but only on Tuesdays, when sizzling
carne al pastor fills the streets
with clarity and the sky
ransoms clouds to the wind
despite their protests that the papers
are in order, we own the real
estate, ni de coña - no nos vais
a

   des

      alo

         jar

so instead we become citrus smears
against the starched blue –
"What does it say?"

               "What does what say?"

"The sky?"

           It says,

"Swell the house with bliss
before the contract expires

and the binding breaks or the pages fall
like bladed leaves, like
burning snow, like walls of paper."
But by Friday
the ground rumbles mutely, Aunt
Dorothy Black looks wistfully out her window
in Belmont Village, sighs "At
last" and lifts herself into evening
dancing her family history into the graceful
arcs and pirouettes of the lightest
ballet - feel the shoes
slide down the steep tremors
teasing them
                  into sweet
                        adagios -
the sky
cannot hold the brushstrokes, the wind
cannot afford the note: follow
her dance
           move
                for move
                      memorize
the choreography until the rhythmic ping
fades into the tender whisper
          of silk
              against wood
and flesh.

The orb-weaver clings to the center of a web
spun between brick and ixora, an asterisk with
crab-like abdomen that lists in the Gulf breeze.
Four silk dots keep linear time below it – slight
asyncopation you would play as a fourth chair
horn trying to match the first chair pace. The brass
bells of the bandroom reflect linoleum and
gloss-covered cinder blocks, celebrate the
long-term tenure of vinyl, nylon, plastic laminate
as their provision becomes the permanent
reel of memory. The students themselves,
like the music, glide with humid breeze
that melds sound and pulse where the gentle
cloud-scuds suggest cloth. Libby and Elizabeth,
my matriarchs, wear the popular sheer hose on Sundays
and even Mondays – its complex molecule chain
retains the living wonder of their legs. Does the
smoothed surface call to us? Or the regulated
structure beneath, the sound of fine-grain friction
resonating with some collective curving of perception
until the belling results when the clapper
strikes the lip and reaches the core of more than
one person? The surface ripples. The warm flush
of afternoon sun disagrees. The sun argues with most
everything, then lays you bare, stripped down
to the flesh in the middle of some occasional
road, suddenly feeling so thankful that you, at
least, can go back to the fresh locked ac of rented
rooms. Like when the bully strikes your lip
and a wider context, a higher authority
steps up to pad the fall – not that justice
will get served, but that you, at least, aren't lost.
See here, as the web tightens, how the wild-grass

flattens then lets up, as if some enormous,
unearthly hand were caressing the gone-to-seed
golf field? Even the grackles harness their purpled
lightning, lizards freeze their head-clicking gears,
and the early summer responds, "Go on,
go on. There's nothing you can weave
that I will not unweave."

Vernal reunions in a pastel
country exceed inner sanctums—
tune the ear to homecoming
and feel the slow tile of balance
restore timidity.

Spread map of spent
movement over flat hours.
Neurotic airplane & topographic trace —
llanura, cuenca, sierra, valle —
then kinetic streets where a film
peels from skin, skin from
another animated ghost
tattering into fog:

Avenida Revolución, El Zócalo,
Coyoacán & El Parque
de Chapultepec – to the south,
Cuernavaca, to the north,
ruins of Teotihuacán. Web
of ghostpaths shaped by bare
feet: lines tracing the age
of palm and lava.

In the metro cars
hot blur of glances,
& a scarce air: pointillistic
impression of identity painted
in massive surges, faces
carved in brilliant relief,
a few islands of conversation,
a curious smile –
seek them out each day,

to hunger and eager
a name to a friend.

Build stones out of bones,
trace blood into solid
architectures of longing,
their buttressed wing
a shade from echo
where the evening takes flight.
But the affinity for structure
fills hunger with walls and squares
until the straight edge breaks down
into volcanic layers. Stand
in the middle of Delegación Benito
Juárez, a pile of rubble
that clatters between seismic rifts.

No longer fluent in the descendent
flesh of words, the parley pattered
with an infinitive overlap,
dressed in a suit of verbs –
not a gentleman so much as an army
of dandelion seeds choking
the pockets, living rooms,
and river valleys of mute
and scarlet resplendent in
mythology.

Dry creek bed of streets
blaze beneath the sun,
tributary of motion,
sky distilled corporally
through the filter
of an overheated town.
Press slow strings,
                    pluck
dire moan from the acoustic
box of late morning
as a car tocks by
missing its muffler.

Sun-baked
            by river bank,
the fog-horned paddlewheel
floats jazz-band
                calliope
                        and passengers –
formal figures recast in shorts
and t-shirts.
                Ohio sludge,
braying mouths,
                passengers
enter the consumable epiphany
of small towns.
                    The ship's manifest
disintegrates until only
the ghosts
                remain.

Early cerulean ache
wicks the present:

                    spurious solvent
wiped into instant
history.

Sun warms sparse grass
                        and bare dirt.

Far to the west, grass grows wilder,
reaches ancient temples,
                            yearns
to mask them,
            once again,
from the profane gaze of tourists.

Riven by century plumes
the runner-ghost of a proto-
nahua family
            weeps
at the sweeping shower,
                        clouds
bursting as they skirt the ruins
carrying the tlaloc downpour
        south.

What moves the bestial sludge
of passion,
            slender arc of
violence,
        the worms
                    that winnow
viral into conversation,

across new-mown clearings

gas pumps
        and Family Dollars?

Slick rage
        paints the monuments,
parks,
     and churches
an indelible shade of
disquiet.

Tear out of sockets
electric sucking
        mouths,
impaling plugs
        with two eyes
and a projectile tongue:

they crave the wiry underworld
and its blue-white streaks
of amphetamine
        crazing the walls,
floorboards,
      air itself. Slap
shut screens, the screaming
signifiers,
       the graphic,
the linguistic,
       the aural:

fantastic junkyard of yeses
and nos
      cannot read
prophecy.

The heart of water
                a eucalyptus
burdened and broken by scour of rain
blows too across
                mountains,
carves the clouds with lingering
remorse,
        with lost friendships
like the whip of electric storms
                    in a soul's glass globe.

Wear the same watch for a decade–
nurse from the dense,
                mechanical
lozenge of metal
virtues of persistence,
                durability.
                      The gears
numbers
        hands
           will still fall
                grasping
at their own face.

Late afternoon sun
gilds unshaded
            half of the pool
as plastic bodies of children
chute down
           the spiral slide
into summer
        burnished by loss.

Float
        towards cool
half-moon
                waters.
Inscribe within
                tiled perimeter
the heads of bathers
                as they press
against tree
            -shaped penumbra.
They test the hour's
                tension
before it gives way
to engulfing bodies. Therein,
look up through
                leaf-filtered blaze,
feel the release,
brief, but   also infinite,
as if the side of the dictionary
                that holds
definition
        fell away,
                leaving only
words,
simple seeds planted anew
                released
                        floating
over pool-blue surface.

§ WEATHERS

The private logon opens spirit hunger,
measures dusk in parts per inch:
lawn green vectors to horizon diminish
the private. Logon opens spirit. Hunger
roots down through windows where hours blemish
until glistening ribcage unfolds elegantly
the password, private logon, open spirit.
Hunger measures dusk in parts per inch.

for Letty

Boiling pasta
        collecting
scattered
                toys
I look up to see your face:

shock of arguments
familiar reconciliations
before a long trip
steel gray rollaboard
packed awry
                toiletries
of motion
                coils
of expansion
                padding
the works with thick
cartilage.

Sharp angles and shadows
of our first courtship
have broadened
                softened –
a comprehension including
weaknesses
                failures
and reservations.

Only when I
walk into our bathroom
and shut the door

            alone with the mess
of product around
                the washbasin
I comprehend
that the remains
contain the entire
                        body:
Aquafresh,
            Old Spice
                        Lancôme
beard trimmer
                curling iron
                        tweezers
maintenance
                compassion
                        nurture.

In the dark stutter of night
hours flash from small displays,
nervous fingers wake up devices
that sleep in sixty seconds.

Outside, ancient rustling
sifts down through oak leaves
and maple branches,
stirs empty streets into morning gravity.

A chronology of turf arranges human force
towards chthonic flows of noon and midnight —
destructions that melt while we work and
sleep, distracted in the old sign systems.

Moving through manicured yards
and those strewn with toys and bare dirt,
pulverizing multitudes gathered
in antique stores, piled in junk shops,

the yawn and groan of inhuman earth
tidal-plowed by amber and copper-
green patinas, lit in submarine blue,
sucks down the goods of dry wit:

fragments of wicker chairs, rotary phone dials,
typewriter platens, die-punches, porcelain-ware,
until they empty out into the river
below town — a disastered

shipwreck of invention expelled
by time's own invented desire —
ghostly inundation with hinges rusted open
scooping the slow current in its trajectory.

The summer storm trails off
into light rain – patters
along pavement releasing smoke
from the heat. Footsteps
outside the warehouse windows
reflect tapping in comic book
bubbles, where innocence
loses itself in a gothic lit
theme park. Between these
scenes the film of humid
afternoon, bloated with oxygen,
carbohydrates and indolence,
peels from the film
of animated pulp:
in the gap
violent laughter
reduces life, affection, affinity
to deadly
punchline.

A reader only sees
frozen angles stomping,
groans scrawled shakily
in the frame; the killing
joke takes meaning
from stark lighting,
green contrasted against
purple, diagonal
streaks of rain
superimpose funpark
with calm drone
of urban night.

Strange chronologies
silver the razor-sharp pain,
slash the comic book frames.
A metronome
wafts through the window
cool and soft,
triangulates nostalgia,
dread,
and chaotic now
where the quiet denouement
of afternoon shower
slants suddenly into
grim carnaval.

Muzzle blasts light up dark corridors
stars fall from eyes
and twinkling death ships
snap into operatic clarity.
Checkered heroes finesse,
then stumble, interred
in charismatic corners
of the spatial plot:
an archetypal clutch
we come to expect.
The story is a trap
of freedom, the story
traps freedom: sunrise
axiom, seditious
sunset, just let
the power of /s/
flow through the mouth
and body – its machines, complex
administrations, billions
of subjects, an inconceivable
tributary
                    [maps of tributaries]

We love you
captive. Favor
a million individualities.
Starve the empire
anonymous – our
rebel, our want.
Rule, this party
rules because
I cannot see my-
self, just a million

recontextualized
justified
yous.
We remember
now
right

       [a million rights]

Dandelion seeds catch
in a web swayed
by afternoon breeze.

The house spider gauges
silk networks
with toothpick legs:

sinister thrums
relay victims' fits
after tangling filament.

But today the lines jitter
with weather and not
spasms toward death.

Later, the seeds' flutter
will loosen, crown gothic
abandon and suspend

ragged decay out-
side the second
floor window pane

where the domestic
arachnid risks
fertile air far

from dirt
or grass.

When winter solstice turns,
the river slows.
It will slow again.

From the alcove
I watch you:
a disaster of peppermint.

Saints with fractured smiles
tread carpets of clover.

You press a silver ring I never gave you
into your palm.

Outside, a pale ferry glides
on ice
across the Ohio.

A shore dotted with lanterns
our grandparents brought
from farms.

I wake you to say
something has happened.
You come to

pissed as hell.

Like a blurred
train sweating diesel

desire tears me
away.

This oak tree rots
in my hands.

Your hair, a golden cloud
that fades in the window.

I never make it to shore.

Ghost-white eye moves within its socket,
glance of recognition trained on neighbors, their
                                        gentle care spread
on children stuttering by the sidewalk, deep
crimson ebb fanned by the memory
                                of lovers.

This was your idea of paradise
I signed up because

                        my inventions failed:

>

like the stainless steel multi-hatch
I programmed to open
                                wherever you did
its magic radar tracking
your born confidence
                                ruddy trust
sensual grippings
                        psychic powers
all soothing as a
                        sweater factory.

But when activated, I emerged
from a portal
                        embedded
                                        in the ocean trench
impossibly compressed
                                single breath
of salt
                and water.

>

Or my version of the happy
                              ending - a kind of
all-purpose snuggie
                        for fate,
sewn to put minor fortunes
at ease
              to luxuriate
                              in the plush
but cumbersome folds
                              sleeves suggesting
both industriousness
                        and somnolence;

a gambit to comfort
                        and restrain
both of us.

>

Or the minor success - a
                        dream ripper:
you fit the long pointy end
                        beneath the thread
that holds the seam
                  of me
                              to you
then let 'er rip.

The blossoms that spring forth
                              red   pink   orange
flood the evening streets

45

and light up

the phantom sockets.

Song of vowels
lamentation of rust
drags its night-silvered wake
through mud-packed shore

a cooper's hollow fear
severs the raft
I struggle, boots thick,
across Beargrass creek

In the shallow bow
your vertigo drifts:
lunar scales
that reel the mind

I search the banks
for the ladder that arches
over polluted murk
and climb

tree bark   silt   barge

    starling   cloud   thunder

Each rung
     a step closer
          to glow

Radiant bouquet of jasmine
slices through cut grass, magnolia,
and honeysuckle haze. Check
weather apps & bolster dopamine
hits: pleasure of anticipating
temperature drops. But the jasmine:
imported from Spain, it lingers
on a framed view of countryside,
painted in whorls, from which night
unfolds and evening lingers–
golden puddles still dissolving
in distant hollows. Dry heat
blown in from the west
dissipates; cool humidity
rolls inland from eastern seas.
Estranged memory recalls
orange blossoms falling
into a river, bright pulp &
jars full of pungent sunlight
bobbing down to sea. One
memory wraps another
like identity & migration–
childhood kernel of sunny chlorine
bound by hard shell of language,
obdurate sarcasm, shame's idiom
burned in a narrow flat
of mature afternoons:
small pitcher of cream, torn
silk along the thigh, armoire
stained in smoky nights
of wine and sweat.
The cobblestones, streetlights,
glass & marble bars fill

the Iberian night — hear its
flamboyant declensions
err on the side of self–
effacement. Stand on this bridge
between jasmine & orange blossom,
watch the current roil water
in optical illusion,
two identities within me
wicking at each other until
personality & translation
become one
chromatic
smear.

The afternoon effluvium
leaves behind wide deltas
of silt & hours;

action slows, traces
spidery erosions & crooked rivulets
through morning grit.
Barometric pressure rises.

Human energy creates
its own diurnal arc,
                        profane spirit
rising through heaving body,
layering work, dinner, play.

House chores sift
through orange blue light
while turbo-diesel engines
craze the ectoplasmic
air on Main Street.

Coughing dogs
& silent owners
appear fleeting.
A sweets shop
chimes open its
door: inside the rich sustain
of chocolate & hard
candy mix with
ozone.

Hours drift & pull
us into the muddied confluence

of tributaries,
                a rickety cove,
muted cartoon violence
from a houseboat trickles
as someone draws heavy blue
curtains aside & peers
out into the evening's
obscure explosion.

A light aftershower
confers shreds of legitimacy
to narrow spectrums
echoed in forecast:
                        radio, tv, webpage,
phone app – mundane filters
magnified through urgency.

In the wet patio across the street
a middle-aged woman, hands on
hips, observes gardening tools,
pots, & mulch
                they glisten & darken
like photographic process.

She wears a white halter-top,
over muscled breasts,
high-cut running shorts,
                        sweatband
lapping forehead;
                paces back
& forth in the wet sheen
smoking cigarettes
& tossing a blond ponytail.

Her athletic, jerseyed intensity
reconciles early evening –
a vessel of time re-encountering
its main current:
delight
                caught lush
in the drift.

Sunday morning
the coffeeshop cook
preps brunch –
beams of eastern light
stream diaphanous
through windows.
Smell of worn wood
rises clean
            from floor...

Cable installers
smoke cigarettes
by their trucks
full of fiber optic
cable & signal boxes —
quiescent transmitters —
as laughter rises
            in the alley...

Pocket of quiet before
Saturday night hangovers
come crashing:
vindications,
            fellowships,
                        hall pews,
then thumping Harley riders
cruise the scenic
highway that splits
            the town...

From roasting coffee
pots of gravy
biscuits   rising

these placeholders
        of stillness
            sheer will

populate
       everywhere
          the day.

The sun-baked GPS
unspools tangled routes
in a vast threadwork —states
of movement unwinding:

Georgia's inherited fields,
the Smokies' blue haze,
the stark Rockies
and roads further than West —

straight off into yonders
where the lens of wealth
pretends not to focus, subjects
shaping identity
free to form —

their dream filters applied to whole
lives, a backward memory: waking
up deep in the narrative to find
the screen blank, to stutter out
loud, "What happened?" Think

of a stained plush bear — once the color
of snow, nose chewed off, burrowing
in the warm crook of late
afternoon beds; a plastic trilogy

of Lego towers, randomly bricked
yellow ‖ red ‖ blue ‖ white, snapping
Saturday morning sun into modular
cuts and flows of pleasure;

a natatorium, long arc into cold water
before dawn, dread sense

in Dagobah swamp,
son's intuition
darkened to discipline,

shadow father slinging
a blazing arc
as his son thrashes
below wavy
aquamarine—

deadly threats
lurk in blind spots, hide
their parallel dimensions
within age-baked densities –

chipped plastic blocks
road markers that
track primary colors
past bear season's plush comfort
into quartz chiclet of chlorine—

unfathomable, total, simple.

That sun-tattered sentence
opens up, finger-stained in the hour
of early dirt, its one thin sentence
of gold and onyx hope
persistent

turned — a growing sense
of freefall suddenly
overtakes the dreamer
and reveals the line of ink crisping
on the long skin of humanity.

I.

That glimmer we make
in a blind slope
scraped from disaster's
layered muck, ignorant
vitriol, compulsive
                information;

that flicker we cup
gently breathe
to catch fire
so that faces, illuminated,
might remember
gestures
                and expressions;

such light eludes –
a failed combustion,
fades back into
obscurity and morass
biological
                soups.

II.

Today, weather tilts
its brief swirl from autumn,
kicks up lacy winter fringe –
numbers drop to freezing
expose chilly
                seductive eaves.

Convalescent wavering
flag of withdrawal
from tobacco, alcohol, cold meds;
the abandonment of streets —
small town agency
windows shuttered
Sorry,
            We're Closed.

Prison bus passes –
inmates clad
raincoat yellow
inside school bus yellow
intermittent flurries
as it pulls away
complex thoughts from
elementary windows
glimmers of language
narrowed
            to a guttering
                      pinpoint.

Hair touches the skin — a brush
of consciousness, breezy & humid
along the fore of someone else's
lilies. Planted before we arrived,
the bulbs nestle and anchor
deep in clay uncertainty.
In this sun-cooked
ranch house a pandemic
abolishes the rules of meals.
Instead, we spread food
across floors and pick our way
from one room
of the day to another.
Weaving through the live oaks
towards us a sunfish reflects
intense scorn for crabgrass.
Above, sitting in the boughs
a tiger smokes, remembering
me from 1983. The dead
possum, clearly smashed
by car tires, looks up warily
and asks, "Haven't you had
enough of your own
ego? It's
killing me." I notice the graffiti
left on the tree boles of the
forest – blanks that pull
bark into them. Leticia backs
away from the doorway, an
unintuitive motion–
like watching VHS in slow reverse
while a conspiracy
theory about Covid-19

plays brashly in the air
behind her. We need
things we need our
things. Brogues clopping
against cobblestones, the gathering
in a small lamp-lit park
celebrating the Dogwood Festival,
the one I left
a hole in, adolescent
denial of my treachery
in this snapshot proof saturated
by a few vivid decades
in which I left
every single friend. Hummingbird,
wasp, and West Indian
Jasmine ease more restrictions,
slow memory tides to the griffon
who springs exhilarated and flies
its desire like Hobbes pouncing
Calvin — or Aida hiding behind
the doorjamb, giggling: one
more mythological surprise.
Our liquid interiors displace us
down a dead-end alley where we
find bleached femur of another alley.
Walk back to the border
and listen to water invent mud –
little death emptying out its end
with nothing behind it, no support –
four empty decades lying down
against a rosy sunset backdrop:
defunct railroad bridge,
sludgy Ohio River, pierced

reflection of skyscrapers
glowing the underbelly
of night.

Fall slips by like a funeral.
Students of the moon attend
silent burials, luminescent families
in obscure worlds. These 8 hour flights with
double feature, thin coffee and atmosphere
charged with no silver disc,
no gravity pull. Another astral body
snuffed, all made of light. *light*

Experts in reflection, we orbit
screens — we make them
sequels to our lives, a continuum
of panel, eye, and experience.
Information fills esophageal sockets,
but the visual gulping
induces vomit, expunging of game scores
troop mvts prices candidates homicides plots
we stretch like a cat in constant convulsion.

Yesterday I recognized
house finch, wren and
tufted titmouse — birds that stay
for winter, active only on my side
of window and field guide. When the source
gives out and our sun reels down to a halt,
the picture ceases its movement,
we are forced to tease the light
out of our own cracked lenses.

I ate my own desire. There where
the mirror reflected fruits, vines,
a sickening pace to rot faster
until the motorcycle slipped
completely off the road. No more
glass dance, the mortgage melted
in my hands, blindingly free
and anchor-less. One more dog-
dripped bark at a pinking moon
and you folded yourself up
in denim forever. The wind
bends trees walls cars sideways
through a prism of salted
prescience, reads the future
homeless sweating and grimed
planting colorful tents
along scythe-curved stretch of beach.
Keep this space for the error,
the botched theory we
millions live by, follow the line
into pavement, dust, cotton bolls,
build beginnings again
from slant sun-ray 2x4s
and the mortar squeezed
from desperation.

Rafts of lumber stacked
to the raftered ceiling
and color-coded
by layer, thickness, particle:
box of parts, box of dreams,
scissor-lifted heavens made of metal.

Take our blue-print prayers and also lift them
from our bodies and our minds,
ecstatic
in their purity of sketch,
lifted to the blue and red
plumbing tubes,
the rainbow-coded electrics,
alabaster columns,
and marble appointments.

Give us this space of liberating light,
divine reflection of form
guarding the ideal:
our life within life's sanctity,
our future bathroom sanctuary.

after Hieronymous Bosch, The Garden of Earthly Delights

Beset by the overriding appetites
of our bodies, the hot humors
rising from our thighs, growing
turgid entering spine, arching us
backward so that our open mouths
search the blackberry in vain,
we hold an eternal gesture
of anticipation. The goldfinch,
stately, fine drawn
and cruel-tipped, gazes blank
at our chicked and nested plaints –
we gawp, mute, wholly invested
from feet plunged in lake-bottom
to the outstretched fingertips
drained of color like the rest
of our flesh, muscle, bone.
The finch holds berry,
power, infinite resource –
is everything, but
completely dispassionate,
offering only
what we cannot reach.
We yearn for the sugary, drugged
infusion of juice
that will again awaken us
to the pounding senses.

Meats heaped
on the creaking table –
plates of rabbit, duck, seared
venison, next to starfruit,
pomegranate blood-popped
and trickling, plantains
half-stripped and heavy,
thick baked carrots, stir-
fried watercress and onion
steeped in sesame seed
oil, sweetbread, sour-
dough, wine
smudged purple across
starch-white tablecloth,
the hard,
pungent
asiago and cheddar,
and clay pitchers of
chilled milk.

Then just as saliva
floods the archways
domes and vaults
of the body
and the steaming
rise of indulgence
bakes braincells
to a splitting fever,
hit delete.

Restless snapshot,
unstill life,
quiz of senses

where teeth bite
a scarlet tongue
appetite:
devour
and digest
infinity.

Plush animals
fade from sofas,
bookshelves, toy chests,
and films - guerrilla
retreat into dark velveteen
taking comfort, caress of flesh
pulp filament,
leaving impressions only,
tigers   monkeys   toucans
persistent negatives
hidden by the foliage
and humidity.

Tired of infiltrating our need
for comfort
as we puzzle their disappearance,
bear   turtle   seal   otter
tune their vital rhythms
and seasonal migrations
to hidden dimensions—
some feed from our kitchens,
some slip into
the shrinking hinterland,
still others adapt to the viral logic
of cities and suburbs,
infesting the wooded roadside,
bumming rides in radiators,
tinting the twilight cathedral
with lurking apprehension —
unanswered questions
hanging in the ruddy, cooling air.

But most vanish

before the age
of interstate highways,
and designer landscapes —
fur   feathers   stitches   buttons
their delicate habits
bleed out filigrees of solace,
despair figures traced into velvet nap
and mud torn grass,
           churned up,
devoured
         by incessant
wormy
mouths.

Dream tatters
flare out
then quiet
in morning periphery.

Statements of blood-tongued
desire & baleful gallop
fade to pure drops of iron & oxygen.

Awake in rectangular dark
unaware of the window
or yard outside window

just self-contained
position

I lean back against pillows
until house & structure,
its system of ducts & wires & tubes,
brings me to myself —
sitting, head-cocking
suburban ac lullaby.

Back in the year
your warm breath
grounded me

simple chore of coffee
I brought to you
made the failure
worth it.

Contrails
slice at sky
where our grins
become chagrin—
aerobatic planes trim wing
& improvise comebacks.

But the fuselage
decomposes,
splinters cloud-blue
as my hand on door knob
closes off the framed breath
between latch & jamb.

How you already know
the evening faked its own atmosphere—
no need, then, to say so.

I turn darkly
into our dark.

On still-dark roads
drivers watch for deer
opossum racoon – fear

the hapless animal
thick in shrub
wooded shadow

before it disasters
the road – a smash
against our hurtling

Flowers open
on slow blade of summer

Air swells with quarrel,
motor, school band discord,
pagan murmurs
of a water-glazed fountain

Brick and
window frame
vacancy:
pigeon speared
on control spikes
fields of maize cracked open
spill and spill
onto county
highway

Maple, elm, oak
spread lucid chorus
alongside river;

nearby, cottonwood
bursts open, summer
snowflakes reflecting on sun

Chromatic metal sleds
at the car show
polished bright and focusing
owners' labors
into nuclei of pain-
staking diligence

Corvette Stingray
shines glossy mirrors
we fill with our sagging
skin billowing
shirts and awe

'66 Nova pushed wide open —
bodywork of Mulsanne blue
releasing metallic-
flaked ash
like a volcano
speeding lava
into chrome crash

for Joey Yates

on a dead end / glass highway / and all my friends are there
— Evergreen.

Where velocity locks doors
down with aching metal
sharpest lights blow night wide open
streaks on your cheek
streaks on your cheek
when the trip
finally hits – world full of
leather-topped soles
treble-laced bass
bet he'll show
up delicate arms pushed
out rolled sleeves push
through other limbs & tatters
deep in chiaroscuro
of house party
now the embrace
now the solace
still within slithering
percussion
when southside, east end, downtown
rub together in the living room
backyard
club bar
no place
not even
memory
to escape
no more
then
76

you can travel you can
shelter you can molder while speed
pulls tiles from your eyes –
thin layer
                    of aluminum
1960s tail-fins skidding
                              piss-pale yellow inside
                                                  holds
panic down
while other drugs limn
                        thin heart's membrane
with sparkling quicksilver
                              grinding locomotive wreck
in forest of cool maple breeze
push your hand in his
                        accelerator mashes sucking down
the fuel all your friends
are there the city
                    spins into solid walls
                                          of light
streetlights spotlights stagelights all your
                                          friends are
there
where you driving
                    feel the walls dis-
integrate where you
                    driving
lightning under toes
                    under tympanum
all the fingers words shouts
                              connecting
through feedback mash
                        hard-stained floors

little ember folded in flannel

                                    he teases translucent

orange glow brighter

                       feel light open

                                          lift

from shoulders like parachute

                              into starless sky

where you going

                  into night

where you driving

           driving

                    where you

                            going where you

driving?

Cars through a fine morning mist
set expectant rhythms;
their percussive conductors
bend silhouettes
over steering wheels, bend into
a solar explosion.
Our addictive behavior
amplifies nature
into a bass note
thrumming deep from earth's crust,
then trebling out through the fx pedals
of cities
and suburbs.
But the sweet chintzy mist
and relaxing drone
root & reach
along the floodplain
for a brief moment play counterpoint
to the human music crescendo,
pulling it down,
and closer
to an unconstructed
harmony.

after artwork by @moon_patrol

Lunar gears grind and build
nocturnal arguments of sorrow
next to my door.

Why wish away the ashen pleat of skin
heavy slough of stillness
marbled over muscle?

Tissue across floor.

Zealous scraps left over in refrigerators.

The past balls up: dirty clothes
forgotten in a derelict house.

My head splits anxious sleep
where I dream my own split sex –
coiffed bob
lake placid eyes
relentless lipstick
sliced by grimy skull
shooting lasers from beneath.

Inside memory,
torture carves out skin slowly.

Open vista rife with forest
thick honeysuckle air
grayed and sapping as we try

to measure the year
until gutted
        charred
                smoked:
pungent heaven
for hobgoblins.

a Mercedes

> *Be for me, like rain,*
> *the getting out*
> —Robert Creeley

Jade chips flake off my overclocked dismay —
verdant little dustpile of memory.

The breakfast daughter came and went,
replete with twenty absent minutes: anniversaries!

Water the bean sprout into magic height,
my daughter runs up and steals desire.

But earth inside plastic inside modular
construction speaks a language deeply internal.

These introverted plants teach no lessons,
just tenacity against bitter winter glass.

What are we that yearn for X or O —
simple forms distracted from nebulous structure?

Once was a time I asked for measured terms
like ancient cobblestone melting under me —

the chalky bridge spanned choking riverbed
while Seville spread around its browns and yellows;

she stood in the warm April afternoon,
sky refusing to water the days and months.

Now years later, I have bought a watch
to hold the rain inside from getting out.

Red maraschino cherries
Stuck in the eye-sockets of an argument
Discord that moves sibilant
Across the clear veneer of Sunday
Flows red where death should grin
Instead a gesture of erasure – hug, or shrug —
A finitude that echoes infinite
Its million grains of sand
Pour out a gaping mouth

This morning the morning was a
blind lurch in a chilled pool. When I
was a child I was a blue plastic car
lost in the bottom of the canal. My
mother was a radiant green window
full of ferns; my father was a horserace.
I am afraid of the end and the paper
crucible of my own skin. *Staring at the sea
staring at the sand.* I love nerves when,
blinded by blood, they cross and
tangle. That winter was a folded
scorch of fireplace tucked between warm
bricks. I left behind the urge to destroy
myself because I was finally good to you.

I wipe clean mantlepiece
polish blank the mirrors
scrape cold ash of fireplace
so the dead starve in their hollow
halls – remembrance
as negative renovation
stripping bare living rooms, patios, and kitchen
into one long corridor:
interior design of
four gray lines
to infinity, almost
touching, a throng
of fading ghosts between.

We please the living – stuff them
with electricity, air conditioning,
computers – their half-life
of milliseconds feverishly tapped
like a chain smoker's faulty lighter
her last ember
already cooling in the gravel.

The wraiths
trail ever on a thinner filament –
always fading
but never
erased.

for Aida Beth, inspired by a dream she had

Thin hour of morning full of gulls
as we walked up the gangplank
in a light breeze that lifted
the smell of home from our shoulders.

We boarded the cruise ship, father,
mother, and me with my cousin
and her parents. The deck moved
slowly below tall masts. I'd never
been on a sailboat before. No one

else was in sight - the white
decks reflected the quiet
sunlight. Emily and I

ran to our cabins
where we threw ourselves
on the stacked bunkbeds
choosing top or bottom
as the dock and large buildings
tilted through the windows.

Water slapped the sides and slipped
far beneath us. A bell rang
and our families left the cabins
through narrow wood passages
to a pair of doors that opened

into a cafeteria bigger
than my whole school, bigger
than a supermarket, and filled

with more people and noise. Two bars
stood in the middle, one for
adults, one for kids. My cousin

and I went to the kids bar
and filled our plates
with frog gummies and roasted goose.
I thought
we must be underwater
and told Emily -

"No silly," she said laughing, "That's
impossible!" By the time
the cruise ended
and we arrived home

I was dead. That's when
my handsome friend Bag
came to our door and gave me
a cell phone. Two days later
it rang — I was invited

to a party. A cardboard maze
filled the yard and I entered:
balloons of red and yellow
floated over my head
and the other kids' laughter
grew dim — there in the papery

passages appeared monsters —
purple ones peering curiously
around the corners, flying ones
floating cautiously as if asking

permission, and ninja ones
showing me elegant ballet
in the soft grass. I made them

all my friends, and together
we approached the center
of the labyrinth
where we heard the earth
slipping away beneath us.

Rhythmic boom of cars passing
recalls past neighborhoods —
slip of dusk through gardens,
loose clank of gate-latch,
pantyhose outlined demurely
in the maplight of a '74 Olds —
all tomorrows will be mountains
that crack & sink. In the rubble
I can never find myself. In my cell-
phone, the mountains persist
& I myself split, fracture, and topple.

Soft whir of naval prop trainers
measures thrumming day. Their
hearts of forged blocks & their aluminum
heads watch us from the skies,
wings spread & fill air
until air itself dissolves
& leaves feather piles
in place of birds flocking.

What violence moves in these machines
that give us a sense of safety?
The swish of crazed
engines streaks sky,
street, & the dirt dreams
of the near dead.

Mother passes through lemon
yellow light Sunday morning,
metallic gray mink coat
through backdoor vestibule
into glitter-blue cadillac: "You

can stay or come, I
don't care anymore."

The women, I will lose
the quiet, stately women.

Heavy snakes rustle boxwoods
then fade into noon. I've already
lost the furrowed men. Brick
sinks dreadful – cornerstones biting
into soft memory, basement
dredges firm slabs deeper
into the porous core
below Mother where her scarlet skirt
whisks between door & jamb:

farewell men, fare-
well women & all the machines
full of ignition & photo-
synthesis. Because of you, I
disappear into the streaked sky.

for Mom and Dad

Ang kita sa bula, sa bula rin mawawala.
(What comes from bubbles will disappear in bubbles.)
Filipino proverb

Dim restaurant interior —
a wood-walled velvety cavern
that seems to crack light
at glass level
where salt crystals flutter to the bottom
of beer sending bubble streams
up frothy surface.
Jim, my father, soaks up the shadows
in a tweed sport coat, leather shoes
I shined the week
before, slate-
gray pants and a squared face
freshly freed
from the O.R.
masks and scrubs,
shakes salt into his drink –
dozens of divers go looking
for wrecks and treasures.
Libby, my mother, presses
against the booth back, her hair
short, coiffed, her white silk
blouse trimmed into cobalt
plaid skirt, hose
the color of flax, deep
red heels – a work
of radiance that would explode
if it weren't written

in discipline
and restraint.
Jim tilts the glass
after a cubed portion of sirloin
and swills away bubble trails – dream
divers foraging the fruits
of thieves & empires.
One Friday after another they balanced
me in the middle at Fifth
Quarter Steakhouse
where I watched the bubbles appear
then disappear
as they filled my mind:

his beer, my Barq's
Full glass
       half glass
             empty glass
Full glass.

Define sumac:
tree, spice, poison,
canopy of unknown
ingredients spilt
under botanic reaches,

brew simmered until gulped
down medicated throat
peristaltic at the bass fever
passing from gate
to inner vestibule –
dirty folded note
tucked behind the ear
of my seventh grade desires – Will,

touch me, Crystal, tongue
me, shock the seeping lagoon
between right eye and
left justification until
the core crackles out
from spine into a thousand
humid gestures —
a drive, a text, a lacuna
that deepens sparkle
blue like Husky pencil,

holds by roots unfolding –
this trace of venom,
sprinkle of seasoning
with dose of excreta, hair
lining tile & Formica edges –

I brace hands

on both sides of the rail
where Crystal sits:
skinny hips marking
her marking me –
we shade kiss we highlight

cheekbones —
bed he & I slept in,
hours inventing
lightspeed futures,
starlit gravities, the arc
& aileron of attraction
between the moons
we knew, a closeness
eroded in time passing –

no fine line no question,
just absent taxonomy
and a blind swagger
in 1985 –
how did we
define it?
            Sumac:
                        blank space
before definition.

Six foot explosion of slender leaves
from a forest island of fleshy
swayed columns
prods thick air with lascivious intent.
Here the Gulf Coast vegetation
grows profligate, an obscene flourish
that devours domestic walls
and subdivided perimeters
beneath heady sun and heavy heat.

Dense green sphere draws in,
absorbs air, oxygen, our frivolous
obsession with presence, leaves
a lenticular procession of transparencies
layering vertically until
a waxy green fills the nose
tapping a collective memory
from 40, then 60, then 80
years ago –

my grand-uncle Dudley
in Puerto Rico leaving the sugar
company office, brushes by the slow
eager bushes framing the entrance.
Flame-orange origami slices
the accumulation of humid
hours that sharpen evening
to a razor red bleed.

I touch the unfolded petals
and feel the cut purse
of mercantile profits
spill through hazy years

when Dudley eased his worry
with balanced figures, stock
prices, careful retirement:
fleeting seagulls
basking in exorbitant rays
that expire beyond
each day's seashore.

Kate Greenaway's compendium
lists lilies for humility, innocence,
majesty, and falsehood;
the red rose for bashful shame
familiar in my own garden —
but nothing on the bird
of paradise, which I can
only define
as calculating sensuality
a guileless presence
that spreads lush fingers
into intimate crooks
and blooms.

Trees interrupt
memory's folded
origami — their gestures
scatter carefully placed
facets of muscle
memory: horse,
monkey, cat, lizard,
python.

A pause in the midst
of forgetting; a
continuum.

Like the water hose
curling from spigot –
stretching its brass 'O'
to base of dogwood –
left mid-chore the
thirstless mouth
continues to irrigate
ravenous pink
blooms.

Chthonic surplus of roots
flex into upheaval
of white oak –
thick gnarly limbs
tower heroically
over pedestrians,
a world of flora
strains to recall each
living being.

Intimate red maple
withdraws gossip into secluded
company, reminds people
the secrets want
                    out.

Burst of verdigris:
prickly lettuce, crab-
grass, pigweed
across sidewalk, lawn,
and driveway – a green

stellar force
interrupting civic history,
rooting its own memory
in ours.

in memory of Elizabeth Ann & Charles Walter Bridgwater

Before Walter leaves the house
for the Louisville L&N train station,
he sits in the den reading the paper
in an olive armchair.
Lady B fixes him eggs, a rasher of bacon,
and hot tea, asks him about the war,
last night's Reds game, or the Beetle Bailey
comic strip. The responses are simple,
heartfelt. Her offerings speak gratitudes,
parsing love into the enameled pan
and simmering with the warm oven.

Their eldest daughter lives in New Orleans,
sends letters and jazz records – the spirits
of Preservation Hall cut into vinyl
and jumping with a metal tide.
Vines of music slink from the parlor speakers
in the evening, charging the mind.
But often the tinny world seems to click
and pulse through the receiver tubes
with an irrelevant glow – sonic wallpaper
that asks too much of the inhabitants.

Their youngest daughter lives in Virginia
Beach with three kids and a husband
somewhere in the Gulf of Tonkin.
She calls Lady B on the phone, talks about
movies seen with the kids, screening
a dustcloud around her personal matters:
John Wayne's epic, single-handed battles,
sweeping cinematics of lonely horse country—

102

she likes to linger on the dancing
ligature of horse and rider. Lady B
easily imagines these captivating pantomimes,
the seduction of an exaggerated solitude,
a real national hero. But she finds the Bible
more graceful: epic storms
and destruction laced
by love stories like spidery
writing cut into rock
with pounding surf.

To live a hundred years, she once told me,
you must know the insignificance
of even one more year,
the pettiness
of a greener dress whose pleats
tumble like rivulets,
of another appliance that opens
new kitchen mysteries,
of the little coffin nailed shut
within a plump retirement plan.
Give freely of your own graces,
she said, expect from tomorrow
nothing more than tomorrow.

100
years since
this disc ticked

warmed
fast against
Walter's pale skin

Silver
case held
slow calvary routine

waiting
training in
Camp Taylor fields

Tarnished
after decades
I squeeze crown

draw
crystal close
face to ear

hear
his measured
routine come alive:

Newspaper
lawn raking
television baseball game

Gears
of solace
grind time down

until
I feel
patient breath whisper

peace
of evening
his mottled skin

move
in unison
with my chores:

tea
cat food
rack-drying dishes

Know his hours
live inside
mine

Windows breathe diaphanous
with sheer curtains Elizabeth
preferred – they respire
drawing in details from other rooms
as if always present:

needlework portrait of Chessie
kitten deep in covers
of a Pullman Car, wheels slipping
pendulous tonnage over rails beneath.
Elgin watch in top drawer – fish
it out, turn crown, replace:
muffled heart memory
of grand-uncle Allen deep
in the chest of drawers.

Metal against porcelain, plastic
rattles glass – she and Walter
finish ablutions in their gleaming,
white-tiled bathroom,
its illumination swallows up
and obliterates the decay.

Walter, a retired train conductor,
collects the careful remains of day
and tucks them with him
into narrow, modest bed.
Feet away, Elizabeth settles
into her own trim mattress,

two atoms bound
in a molecule of room.

Turn in as the engine rumble
grows south of Preston
Highway. Early summer enters
and leaves through the open
window, over the back yard
where iron rails cut grass edge.
Billow of gauze amplifies night,
then blare and squeal
of diesel steel
lulling your
childhood
asleep.

Still evening descends
drapes the maple bordered
triangle park that faces
a trim and reserved
two story brick house

From a front pocket Walter
pulls a worn white
plastic vial
half-full of saccharine tablets
heldover from the WWI
sugar shortage

runs a hand across
bald mottled pate
drops two into
tea cup

I rub lace covered
sofa arms, watch Elizabeth
settle tartan wool skirt
soft against metal
radiator cabinet

Later, walking home
the jar of tomato sauce
I collected for Mom
slips
stains sidewalk
in a glass blood
splash

Blue billy goat weed tucked in mud
blinks at me
damp green undergrowth
and earthy bracken along riverbank

My daughter's croupy cough
accompanies us
on our idle path

Later, I have to look up
the adamant, blue name:
billy goat weed

But back in the moment, bright
pubescent petals
with trumpeting stamen
hold my attention

Narrow leaves mud-streaked
dark green
crowned by
spherical blue luminosities
grown careless along the path

AB wants to pick some
but I stay the impulse to tear
and gather

The weed tenuates perception
with no name, no
understanding, offers
only experience

a lonely
beautiful frustration

Up the river
up mountain
halos rise lenticular
& brambles choke canyon
with fallen mortality —
struck canyon | strike canyon.
Moonglow floods a silver
frosting on each sharp edge.
If I had another
milk-pale disc
to slip between your ears
I'd still lose it in the filth
& flotsam unravelling
in this swollen river —
its serpentine froth
full of undercuts, eddy lines
& washed-out hydraulics –
Ambien & bourbon
cycles keep turning
into simple straight lines —
gridded forest flashing
deep leaf tunnels as the
Oldsmobile station wagon
slips past. I always thought
a river erodes the body
but in a single headlamp
strapped to head or held in hand
other satellites, focii, focos,
reveal themselves – just
like that, *foco*, as in torch
or flashlight
sweeping the forest floor
then highway & finally

a weed-hatched parking lot:
abstract like a painting
in an art gallery – Rothko
on weeds, but something
Wal-Mart vast.
Then brilliant penumbras
sweep into suburbs,
operators looking for signs,
hope, deer eyes
trace the outline of electricity
yards-long shadows
slat out of fences – rails
for jails, *cárcel* = a car
with its cell: something
mobile that seems
to move only from the inside.
And finally the one lung
hung blue & radiant
in night, like sapphire
just beyond the only intersection
(everything else premium
fencing, gates, and lawn
architecture for miles).
Hung there as if
on trial
as if the last generator
plugged into viscera
pumping our veins with beams
of light, *luz*, playing off it
the *z* spreading out
into the neighborhood
respirando, drawing everything
into the blue furnace.

Return – not round trip

                              nor one way

                                            but curlicues

                            in a spring,

vocations of simplicity twining

                                    complicated professions

dawn gazer

                gardener of intuitions

                                      downpour douser

homemaker

                  medical doctor

                          schoolteacher.

Dank cellar shelves

                        lined in glass jars

sunset peach

                  raspberry heart

                                  ocean-bottom grape

                  honey-ray apple

a rainbow preserve.

In another house

                      glass-eyed cabinets hold

snaked stethoscopes

                        meat-wedge reflex hammer

                                          glistening

syringe

                      dream & sleep swimming vials

flat-toothed forceps.

Teacher

                housewife

                        physician

                                        these
faded phantoms
each year travel the far
                        open country –
                                        tucked behind
                mountain range.
They approach home
                        from the backyard.
I bring out a pot-bellied carafe
                                of sweet tea
we sit on the porch,
                wicker chairs,
                                        mosquito screens
                and the glass sweats
into the calm afternoon.

They tell me:
cup the stray bullet
                        breath on it
                                with patient fragrance;
build your inner sanctum
                        with magnolia integrity
                                                hand
soaps
                                and routine mirrors.
Let the patient speak
                she knows the secret channels
                                                vessels
make.
                Stay away
from hospitals.

Each year I nod,

                    thank them,
then wash the pitcher
                              in the sink
                                          guard it
                    safely in its cabinet
and watch them disappear
                              ghosts together
                                                back into
mountains.

Deepest thanks to Leticia Bajuyo for the use of the image of her sculpture, "Two-Story Excavation," and for helping to design the cover.

Sincere gratitude to the following publications, in which previous versions of these poems appeared:

Amarillo Bay: "Bird of Paradise"
Corpus Christi Writers Anthology 2018: "Song of the Signal Path," "Tool for Feeding the Flood"
Corpus Christi Writers Anthology 2020: "Stall Turn"
    Corpus Christi Writers Anthology 2021: "A Hundred Years," "Song for Ravaged Youth," "Tool for Waking the Dreamer"
Corpus Christi Writers Anthology 2022: "Map of Storm," "Spirit Browser," "Tool for Shedding Skin," "Window Veil"
The Dillydoun Review: "Between Us"
Drunk Monkeys: "Moon Patrol"
EM Literary: "Cinephile"
(in parentheses): "Map of Empty Mirrors," "Song of the Sumac," "Tool for Transmission"
Miracle Monacle: "Tool for Interior Displacement," Vagary Ships"
Noble/Gas Qrtly: "Canción sevillana"
San Antonio Express: "Parts Prayer: Aisle 2"
San Antonio Review: "Heat Mirage," "Map of Chorus," "Map of the Remains," "Tool for Ghost Drafting"
Sybil Journal: "Song for Wintering the Solstice"
Tiny Seed Literary Journal: "Adamant"
Voices de la Luna: "Fluid Phylum," "Morning Was a Blind," "Orb-Weaver," "Skull Oracle"
Windward Review: "Hanna," "In the Swash Zone," "Subtropical Herbarium"

I owe a great debt to many people in acknowledging the inspirations, encouragements, support, and context of this collection. First and foremost, none of this would exist without my spouse, Leticia Bajuyo: her energy, artistry, stability, and optimism provided the most vital elements in creating the art I manage to capture in these pages — all my love and gratitude to her. Many mentors, guides, and teachers have played pivotal roles in helping to create poems herein. I would like to especially acknowledge Cynthia Cruz and the support of her online workshops, where many of these poems originated; Natalie Shapero and her inspiring Kenyon Summer poetry workshop; and, Dr. Melissa Dinverno's passion for poetry, language, and teaching in the Spanish Graduate program at Indiana University continues to provide me with a beacon to approaching literature and the classroom. I am deeply grateful to the faculty at Texas State University's MFA program, especially Cyrus Cassells, Cecily Parks, Kathleen Peirce, Steve Wilson, and Naomi Shihab Nye: their challenging and inspiring mentorship fed directly into the composition and revision of these poems. My peers and fellow writers in this MFA program infused the atmosphere with vital energies and conversations, for which I am grateful. Robin Carstensen has provided wonderful support, friendship, and opportunity, along with so many others in the Corpus Christi, TX scene: Tom Murphy, Sarah Lenz, Javier Villarreal, Alan Berecka, Sister Lou Ella Hickman, Juan Manuel Pérez, Nick Carbó, and many others in connection with the Peoples Poetry Festival (now Peoples Literary Festival). I especially thank Bill and Carol Mays and their efforts at putting together and publishing an annual writers' anthology that promoted a diverse range of work and voices from the coastal region through their *Corpus Christi Writers Anthology*. Furthermore, I would like to recognize pivotal inspirations whose work I deeply admired, read, or listened to in the process of composing this collection: Michael Burkard, Cynthia Cruz, Natalie Shapero, Rachel Blau DuPlessis, Julie Doxsee, Leopoldo María Panero, Federico García Lorca, Dylan Thomas, Mogwai, Explosions in the Sky, Mono, Parlour, Sigur Rós, This Will Destroy You, Los Punsetes, El Columpio Asesino, Death Grips, Dirty Beaches, Fugazi, Louisville bands from the 90s [Crain, Slint, Rodan, Evergreen, Sunspring, The Loved, Undermine, Rachel's], Fluxus, Zaj, Fernando Millán, Poesía N.O. The role of dear friends and companions in the pursuit of art, literature, and life exerts a special effect in anything good I might do, especially Joey Yates, Naomi Stuecker, Mark Long, Sarah Evans Murray, and Andrea and Chris Hempstead. A most sincere and essential gratitude goes to Karen Cline-Tardiff for being such a wonderful editor, for seeing something in these poems, and for the work she does at Gnashing Teeth Publishing. Finally, ocean-deep thanks to my family, who may not understand me all the time, but never cease to accept and support me: my Mom, Elizabeth Bridgwater Hamilton, my siblings, Mark, Beth, Ellen, and my daughter Aida Beth — love to you all.

Joshua Bridgwater Hamilton is a Louisville, KY native who lives in Norman, OK. Between Kentucky and Oklahoma, he has traveled and lived in several places, including Spain, Appalachia, Panamá, Peru, the Philippines, the Colorado River, and Texas. He earned a BA in English and Humanities and an MA in Spanish from the University of Louisville, holds a doctorate in Spanish with Indiana University, and is currently an MFA Poetry candidate at Texas State University. Joshua has worked as a dishwasher, barista, bookseller, and currently teaches He has two chapbooks: *Rain Minnows* with Gnashing Teeth Publishing and *Slow Wind* with Finishing Line Press. His poetry appears in such journals as *Windward Review, Voices de la Luna, Tiny Seed Journal, Amarillo Bay, The Dillydoun Review* and *San Antonio Review.*